STAR POWER

by Daphne Greaves
illustrated by Kevin Rechin

SCHOOL PUBLISHERS

Printed in China

ISBN 10: 0-15-350517-6
ISBN 13: 978-0-15-350517-1

Ordering Options
ISBN 10: 0-15-350334-3 (Grade 4 Below-Level Collection)
ISBN 13: 978-0-15-350334-4 (Grade 4 Below-Level Collection)
ISBN 10: 0-15-357507-7 (package of 5)
ISBN 13: 978-0-15-357507-5 (package of 5)

5 6 7 8 9 10   985   12 11 10 09

Characters

Narrator 1
Narrator 2
Lauren
Person 1
Person 2
Astronomer
Copernicus
Galileo

Setting: A fourth-grade classroom

Narrator 1: Get ready to travel back in time!

Narrator 2: Learn about the sun, planets, and stars.

Narrator 2: Our fourth-grade class presents "Star Power: A History of Astronomy."

Narrator 1: Now who is this headed our way?

Narrator 2: Don't you recognize Lauren? She's in your reading group.

Narrator 1: Of course I recognize Lauren. She's supposed to be an astronomer!

Narrator 2: Oh, what am I saying? That isn't Lauren. That's an astronomer.

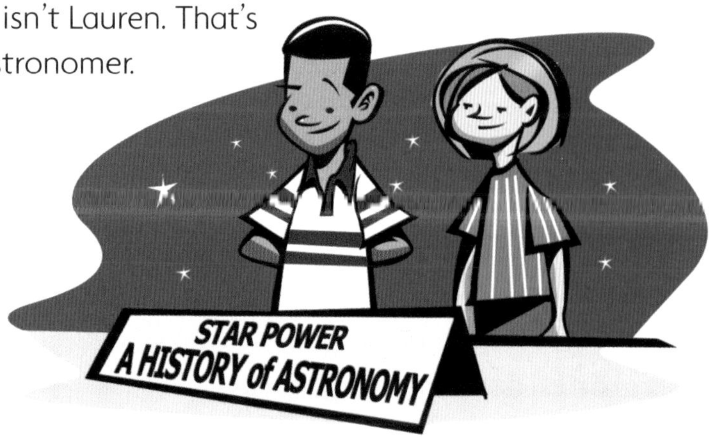
STAR POWER
A HISTORY of ASTRONOMY

Lauren: That's right. I am an astronomer.

Narrator 1: Could you give us some background about the science of astronomy?

Lauren: Astronomy is the study of the universe. Our planet, Earth, is part of a solar system in the universe. The solar system includes other planets that encircle the sun. The sun is really a star. Did you know that there are billions and billions of stars in the universe?

Narrator 2: That's a lot of stars!

Lauren: It is, so I should really get back to work now.

Narrator 1: Thanks for stopping by.

Narrator 2: Billions and billions of stars. That's impressive.

Narrator 1: Here's another impressive fact. Astronomy is the oldest science.

Narrator 2: Does that mean it's time to go back to the past?

Narrator 1: It sure does. Stay flexible! You have to be pretty pliable and quite nimble to make this trip! Hold on!

Narrator 2: That was quite a trip. Who are those people lumbering around? They look kind of primitive, don't you think?

Narrator 1: Of course they're primitive. We are now thousands of years in the past. Look, they are pointing and looking at the sky. Let's listen.

Person 1: *OOGA!*

Person 2: *ULA!*

Narrator 2: What are they saying?

Narrator 1: The first one said, "Look!" Then the second one said, "Cool." Now they are scanning the sky.

Persons 1 and 2: *AAG OOK IBA ULU OOBA WOOG.*

Narrator 2: Now what are they saying?

Narrator 1: "The stars look like they are moving. Let's watch."

Narrator 2: So that's really how the science of astronomy began?

Narrator 1: That's right. When ancient people inspected the stars, they noticed that the stars moved in repeating patterns. They used these movements to mark time.

Narrator 2: You mean they used the stars like a giant calendar?

Narrator 1: Something like that. Anyway, ancient people made calendars by watching the stars. They planted and harvested crops based on where the stars were in the sky.

Narrator 2: Maybe those people weren't as primitive as they looked.

Narrator 1: Maybe not. As the centuries passed, astronomers untangled more and more secrets of the universe. Let's move ahead a few thousand years.

Narrator 2: What's going on? What are you astronomers arguing about?

Astronomer: Just the usual. Astronomers can be so loud.

Narrator 1: Who are you?

Astronomer: I am an ancient Greek astronomer. I'm not trying to brag, but the Greeks made many important and unique contributions to astronomy. Do you believe me?

Narrator 2: Sure, I believe you.

Astronomer: Well, don't just believe me. Believe Homer!

Narrator 2: Who was Homer?

Narrator 1: Homer was a poet in ancient Greece.

Astronomer: He wrote a famous poem in the eighth century B.C. It even mentions constellations!

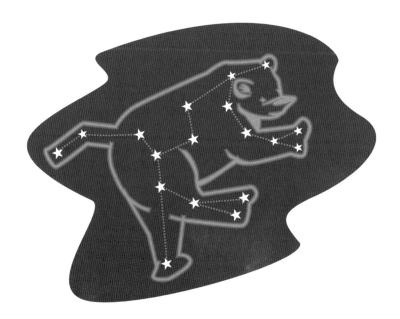

Narrator I: Constellations are groups of stars like the Great Bear and Orion.

Astronomer: It's an inspiring poem. Would you like to hear it?

Copernicus: Not that poem again! Listen, most of you thought the Earth was the center of the universe. Why can't you comprehend this? It isn't!

Narrator 2: Who's he?

Copernicus: I am Nicolaus Copernicus!

Narrator I: Wow! What a pleasure, sir.

Copernicus: You've heard of me?

Narrator I: Of course! You're a great astronomer.

Copernicus: That's very nice of you to say.

Narrator 1: Copernicus was born in 1473.

Narrator 2: He wrote an important book. It said that the Earth moved around the sun.

Astronomer: Big deal! It wasn't exactly a best seller. Now Homer's poem—that was a hit!

Copernicus: If I hear one more word about that poem!

Galileo: Calm down, Nicolaus. There's no need to feel vulnerable or to get your delicate feelings hurt about that poem.

Narrator 2: Now who is *he*?

Narrator 1: I'm not sure.

Galileo: You know, Copernicus, until me, nobody paid any attention to your theory that the Earth moved around the sun.

Narrator 1: Wow, are you Galileo?

Galileo: The one and only.

Narrator 1: Galileo was another great astronomer.

Narrator 2: How did you get people to pay attention to what Copernicus said?

Galileo: I discovered proof to support his theory that the Earth revolves around the sun.

Astronomer: That is great! Now can I read Homer's poem?

Copernicus: Not that poem, please!

Galileo: Please, can't we cease this behavior and act like mature scientists!

Narrator 2: The astronomer guy was right. Astronomers are loud and reluctant to get along!

Narrator 1: Let's go back to the present.

Narrator 2: Great idea! Hold on! Here we go!

Narrator I: It's good to be back. Did you learn anything from our trip?

Narrator 2: I sure did. Astronomers are a pretty exuberant bunch!

Narrator I: I learned that it takes more than a solitary scientist to nurture an idea.

Narrator 2: Huh?

Narrator I: I'm just saying that people like the Greeks, Copernicus, and Galileo all helped us understand the universe. I think that's exciting!

Narrator 2: You know something? You're pretty exuberant, too.

Narrator I: Maybe we should wrap things up.

Narrator 2: Let's see whether Lauren will talk to us.

Narrator I: Who?

Narrator 2: Not Lauren, I mean the astronomer.

Narrator 1: That's better.

Lauren: You wanted to talk to me?

Narrator 2: We just wanted you to say a few words about modern astronomy.

Lauren: Okay. Today's astronomers use powerful telescopes, cameras, and computers to study the universe. Like ancient people, they are fascinated by what they see and learn.

Narrator 2: Thanks a lot, Lauren—I mean thanks a lot to our astronomer.

Narrator 1: We hope you've enjoyed "Star Power: A History of Astronomy."

Think Critically

1. What is the overall topic of the students' presentation?

2. What does the word *vulnerable* on page 10 mean? Why is Copernicus feeling vulnerable?

3. How do the narrators solve the problem of being around the noisy astronomers?

4. Why does the author have the narrators go back in time?

5. What was your favorite part of this Readers' Theater? Why?

🍁 Science

Famous Astronomers In this Readers' Theater, you learned about two famous astronomers. Go to the library or on the Internet and research Copernicus or Galileo. Write down five facts about the astronomer.

 School-Home Connection Read this Readers' Theater with a family member. Observe the sun throughout the day. Notice how the sun appears to travel across the sky.

Word Count: 1,032